Everything About Everything

If information is power,
why aren't we more powerful?

or

Everything About Everything

. . . .

A futuristic tale about infocentricity
and a young man with a nose for
information and an inquiring mind.

An inspirational text about
information recycling and reuse.

. . . .

by

Anthony C. Constable

First Edition: July 2011

Printed in the U.S.A.

ISBN 978-0-9837088-0-3

Published by:
Avenue Design, Inc.
P.O. Box 512 • Fort Bragg, California 95437
www.avenue-design.com

Contents

Foreword – 1995

Most of us can remember first setting foot in the world of work. The place had a look, feel, and ambiance that was different from anything we had experienced hitherto. People in this curiously busy environment dressed and acted appropriately; phones rang and were answered, typewriters tapped out their distinctive cadences, and paper, mounds of it, was everywhere.

In my case, the year was 1958. Within my father's time, office people could only communicate face-to-face or by means of paper. The telephone and postal service were the sole means of communicating with the outside world. The computer was still largely science fiction—the ledger and pen were the back office tools of necessity and choice.

Contrast my experience with that of the present day teenager. Teenagers around me are more computer literate than some of my colleagues and most of my peers. Today, it is a fact that home computer use is at least as advanced as it is in the average office environment.

What helped push the home computer into the status of "appliance" was more the computer-based video game, not word processing, electronic spreadsheets, and database capabilities. As games became more sophisticated, platform and peripheral requirements grew. As the availability of platforms and peripherals grew, so did the products and offerings that expand their use. This process will continue— there is no end in sight. Many of today's toys have become intangibles—perhaps we should call this "virtual" unreality.

My belief is that the sophistication of today's youth in home and school computer use is rapidly eclipsing that of the commercial world. Moreover, and here is the key issue, the way youth uses, shares, and reuses information is a model that should be emulated by enterprises of all types. As today and tomorrow's youth make their transition to the work force, they will increasingly experience culture shock at the hands of a widening home-to-work technology and sophistication gap. As we race toward an economy dominated by services, several issues arise, chief among which is the question: *Why would bright, young, computer literate people want to join enterprises that are in the technological and informational Dark Ages?*

The purpose of this text is to show enterprise managers why they must reinvent their activities, not only to remain competitive in the information-efficient world of tomorrow, but also to attract and retain their next generation of talent.

Fast Forward to 2011

Since this fable was written in 1995, little related to information has changed. Enterprises of all sorts still don't know what information they do know, and many fail to see the value or importance of trying to remedy this situation.

Notwithstanding, I still see the embrace of information husbanding as the *next big thing* for the IT industry. Today, even with Google and its peers, IT is still 99% about technology and 1% about information. To change this will require a change to the underlying culture. When this change happens, we may even see corporate balance sheets including pre-positioned information as a corporate asset, much as inventories and other tangibles are valued.

So, even though the world has been slow to develop a desire to stop paying to learn the same information over and over again, my company, CAI/SISCo, has been practicing what we preach and reaping the reward. Husbanding and leveraging our pre-positioned information has reduced our competitive analysis and price to win (PTW) project costs and prices by at least 20%, allowing us to increase market share without increasing head count.

Acknowledgements

"Between the idea And the reality
Between the motion And the act
Falls the shadow. . ."
—T.S. Eliot, The Hollow Men, 1925

This book is dedicated to:

My son John, whose society was the model for Mark.

My colleagues at CAI/SISCo, who have for years humored me as we pursue this and other visions.

Susan Shealer, who edited this text.

My customers who have come to see the future, have believed, yet almost always have failed to take the first few steps. (Perhaps my powers of persuasion are inadequate?)

The unknown cartoonist whose work (below) I have enjoyed for a long time.

True knowledge workers everywhere who labor to spread the word and the wealth, yet often end up feeling like the salesman in the cartoon.

"No, I can't be bothered to see any crazy salesman. We've got a battle to fight."

CHAPTER ONE

The Invitation

In early August 2004, Mark Wonder was skipping electronically through a science fiction novel that he had downloaded from an electronic book service in Alaska. The story told of a species of intelligent life that had invaded earth to feed on silicon chips embedded in Earthling computers. It was early afternoon on this hot day when the telephony window on his computer screen blinked, indicating that there was a general house call. The old fashioned audible phone in the next room also sounded, but Mark had little use for it since computer-integrated telephony became available. He glanced at the caller ID panel, which told him the call originated at Wonder Enterprises in New Jersey, so he positioned the cursor on the screen's *respond* button using a headband-mounted pointer, blinked his right eye twice to answer and activate *record* and said "Hello, Wonder residence."

"Hi there, Mark," said a familiar voice that Mark noticed also had a by now familiar visual dynamic range pattern. "How's my computer-genius grandson?"

Mark had long-since become accustomed to being thought of as the family's computer nerd-in-residence. Strange though, he often mused, how most people think that you have to be bright to use computers rather than that you have to be rather dull not to. A computer user since the age of three, Mark had seen computer friendliness improve rapidly to a point where they really do make doing more with information both possible and easy. The awe, he thought, should be showered on guys like Shakespeare who had researched and turned out prodigious quantities of high quality work without even the benefit of a typewriter!

During his previous semester, Mark had analyzed the complete works of Shakespeare, which he had downloaded from the local library, and found that it contained 4,357 unique words—a fantastic vocabulary for anyone in the early 2000s, let alone the early 1600s. To do so, he had had to call the library's electronic information number, browse through the offerings, select the Shakespeare offering, and click a button on his screen to set the transfer going, all while on the video phone to his friend Alex. If that is today's version of a genius, he mused, we are in serious trouble.

"Hi Gramps, how are you?" Mark replied.

"I'm fine, thanks. How's your vacation?"

Mark relayed that while vacation had been a welcome break, he was now anxious to get going on his final year in graduate school.

"Well Gramps, I'm afraid everyone else is out right now," said Mark.

"No problem." was the reply. "I called to talk to you, anyhow."

Mark's grandfather described how he would like to show Mark around Wonder Enterprises, the family novelty item business, and begin introducing the concept of joining the firm and thinking about maybe, one day, running it. Mark, having already sailed, fished, swum, and relaxed away several weeks at the family's lakeside cabin, jumped at the chance to look into something new. He had never really had the opportunity to understand the company that employed many of his relatives—the prospect excited him. Arrangements were made for the following Tuesday when Mark's grandfather would stop by to pick him up at 7:30 A.M. Mark was to tour Wonder Enterprises operation in the morning, eat lunch in the cafeteria, and journey back home in the mid afternoon.

"Look forward to it then," said grandfather. "I will put an information packet in the mail to prepare you for the sorts of things you will be seeing—what we do, how we function, and why our customers need us. This will give you the opportunity to quickly develop some insights and ask informed questions."

• • •

As Mark initiated the *terminate* mode and was logging a spoken description of the arrangement into his personal scheduler/calendar, he regretted not having asked for soft copy or even facsimile versions that he could have interpreted into usable/reusable information. But he knew it would have been fruitless. He had long since given up trying to understand why hard copy items such as brochures were still published when the information they contain would be infinitely more useful in a computer-usable form. It must be a hold-over from the "publish or perish" mentality that had created the information "landfill" that he perceived was now plaguing academia.

Mark had discovered early in academic life that the big secret to accomplishing and scoring high on many homework assignments lay in tapping into pre-existing databases. Many scholarly information sets were accessible through the school's computer lab while access to others was available through the subscription to the so-called Super Files that his parents had given him last Christmas. Activating the communications window, he directed the system to connect to *The Revelator*, the popular information service to which he spoke his password (it picked up his voice print as well as his code). He quickly navigated to corporate information and within seconds had downloaded everything that the system had on Wonder Enterprises.

Mark and his friends had long stopped using the telephone for intercommunication. They preferred instead the multimedia approach that had become available. With its full motion video, music, and other personalizations to spice up the conversation, Mark quickly established a video teleconference with his buddies and told them what he wanted.

Within minutes Mark received information on Wonder Enterprises from several other electronic sources, including all SEC filings, and was now ready to analyze it using his All Source Analysis System (ASAS). When Mark returned from getting himself a drink, ASAS had combined all of his Wonder Enterprises information and reduced it to a single non-repetitive set. Mark activated the *Topic* option and within seconds the entire information set was displayed as an inverted tree. The top of the inverted tree showed the topics that had occurred most frequently while the leaf position presented least frequent occurrences. This weighted analysis presented Mark with an extremely detailed picture of Wonder Enterprises from which he then developed some questions.

• • •

Sure enough, the next day's mail brought Mark a fat packet of impressive-looking multicolored brochures describing the company, its recent performance, products, and philosophy. Some contained pictures of people working with '80s vintage computers and other electronic apparatus, groups in animated postures viewing diagrams and reports, and serious-looking manager/executives including, he noted, his uncle John Wonder, President of Wonder Enterprises, and of course his grandfather, company founder and now Chairman of the Board.

CHAPTER TWO

The Day Begins

"Good morning, Mark." A mellifluous female voice super-imposed over mild applause sounded from the bedside computer. "It is Tuesday, August 14, 2004. Eastern Standard Time is 0645. The temperature is 20° Celsius, that is, divide by 5, multiply by 9 and add 32, 68° under the now obsolete Fahrenheit system." The voice continued with a short weather report and news headlines that the computer had recorded from the 0630 News. "Your calendar shows that you will be visiting Wonder Enterprises today. You must be ready to leave at 0730."

"That's all darling. Have a nice day. Don't forget to make your bed and, oh yes, wash behind your ears won't you?" the voice taunted.

"I must remember to give that thing a lobotomy," Mark mumbled as he rose.

By the time he had dressed, retrieved the leather attaché case that was already packed with the Wonder Enterprises brochures and his PDA onto which he had already down-loaded his analysis of the company, a car horn was sounding in the driveway. He greeted his surprised sister and parents downstairs in the kitchen and, while making for the door, his mouth full of warm marmaladed toast washed down with gulps of orange juice, explained his forthcoming day.

"Morning Gramps, ready when you are," he said as he slid in the passenger seat of the car beside his grandfather while the seat belts settled around him.

Riding to the company, Mark listened with interest to his Grandfather's account of how the company was started in the late 1950s, growing from humble beginnings to become a major novelty item concern.

"Of course," Grandfather Wonder continued, "things were very different then. We have always had a steady market for our Groucho Marx disguise kits, Whoopee cushions, and squirting lapel flowers, but that market is limited. The real success lies in predicting the whims of the public. We made lots of money with Dan Quayle Mr. Potato Head dolls, that is with an . . .OE, which were big in 1990, as were George H. W. Bush lips adorned with the *No New Taxes* legend."

"In the early days, we had to do things the hard way," he continued. "We had no fax machines, computers, or any of the other things your generation can't seem to function without. We had to *remember* everything about the business; the customers, the items they wanted, how much we charged them. . .everything! In fact, I prided myself on knowing everything there was to know about the company—it was a matter of survival. Of course, today, we have computers to do those sorts of things. Even so, Mark, I still try to keep the company up here," he said tapping his forehead.

Mark thought about this for a while. "You mean that you try to remember information about 5,000 customers, world-wide, over 2,000 novelty products, and about 500 employees?"

"Ah Mark," was the reply, "when you're in business, you must remember everything that is key to your business. Take customers, for instance. They are the real strength of any enterprise. However, you always have to remember that each one is different and they have a right to be treated as such. A case in point is old George Formby at Party Politics, one of our very best customers, a weird bird. If you happen to ask for decaffeinated coffee when you call on him he delivers a long lecture on the evils of tampering with Mother Nature and, after you've gone, cancels all of his orders with you and has you struck off his supplier list. Where would we be if I weren't around to tell that to everyone who deals with their account!"

"I see what you're getting at Gramps," Mark said carefully. "However, since none of us can be anywhere at all times, trying to remember everything can't be the best solution. For instance, who warns people about George Formby's foibles when you're off on a long fishing trip?"

"That's a good point Mark," said Granddad. "Imperfection is indeed alive and well. However, there's no way around that, is there?"

"Funny you should say that," said Mark. "It so happens that there is."

Mark went on to describe a concept that he had come across in an electronic book a friend had mailed him some months earlier. The concept questioned why human beings tend to clutter their minds with information that they repeat over and over again as a response to some sort of trigger. Instead, so the theory went, enterprises should utilize existing information infrastructures—a "corporate" memory—and the means for capturing and sharing information and having it pre-positioned for possible reuse. The concept, (promulgated in the late 1980s by a company called CAI/SISCo in Frederick, Maryland) is called infocentricity, the word coined to describe the metamorphosis from sole-reliance on unreliable human memories to a shared and very reliable institutional memory that is available 24 hours a day, seven days a week. The thesis behind this concept boils down to: *While people may think, only computers can truly remember everything.*

After a period of silence, Grandfather said, "You're a piece of work, aren't you? In your usual roundabout way, you're telling me that a computer system could easily remember and inform everyone about George's idiosyncrasy. Gee, if one pursues that line of thinking to its logical conclusion, old Gramps will be out of a job!"

"Not so, and far otherwise," Mark responded. "It is true that you would no longer be needed to remember these things once you had told them to the system. However, then you would be free to do what people are really good at: thinking. Everything that you know would be available to all other Wonder employees and, this is the really good part—everything that they know would be available to you."

As the car drew up in front of the gates of Wonder Enterprises, the senior Wonder gesticulated toward the complex of buildings beyond and said, "You know Mark, if the company ends up being yours, you too will pretty much need to know everything about everything."

Mark, by now, was intrigued.

CHAPTER THREE

At The Office

They arrived at Mr. Wonder's oak paneled presidential office. While his grandfather attended to communications that had come in from all over the world during the night, Mark busied himself with the array of mostly familiar novelty items that were exhibited museum-style in a large lighted display case. For as long as he could remember, items like these had appeared at family gatherings to amuse both the children and the adults.

The office was furnished with a lounge grouping, a six-person conference table, a large clockwork timepiece, several exquisite oil paintings, and his grandfather's imposing desk. Apart from the wireless telephone cradles placed around the room amidst other desktop paraphernalia, the place was timeless. Not a computer in sight.

Mark turned his attention to his grandfather, who was reading through a small pile of fax paper, occasionally pausing to scribble a note on a yellow sticky pad, attach the note to a particular fax, and carefully place the resulting document on one of three developing piles.

Mark was amazed. "Gramps, I thought those sticky pads and paper faxes only existed in old movies," he exclaimed. "Nowadays I thought everyone in the business world read incoming communications from voice activated e-mail and recorded their comments and ideas with commands to electronically distribute, file, or discard the results. That way, you can at least make sure that people receive and read the things you send them! What's even better, though, is that you can remember as a by-product all of your random thoughts and impressions and make them available to your knowledge worker community for use or re-use. It really is the way to go."

"My people take care of those sorts of things," Mr. Wonder replied presidentially. "Besides, someone in my position looks foolish playing with the sort of electronic gadgetry that you young guys can't seem to live without."

"Well Gramps," Mark started, "as the company's key knowledge worker, don't you need to both receive inputs and provide direction? What you know is referred to as 'intellectual capital' nowadays, and it should be made more widely available to your people. Why, dealing with these faxes electronically could be so much more productive both for you and your people. As the captain of this rather large corporate ship, you are responsible for making myriad minute course corrections that add up to a distinct direction. I hate to preach, but by using a modern enterprise navigation system, you could do more in less time. What you're doing is the marine equivalent of using a personal compass that only you understand and communicating course change orders and other ideas on yellow stickies."

"Mark, you've got to realize I'm a busy man," the old man said somewhat condescendingly, "I just have never had the time to fool around with computers."

"Of course you're busy," Mark responded somewhat angrily, "and that is precisely why you could benefit from the sort of electronic assistance you presume I 'play' with. It is true that 'virtual reality' video games were an early passion of mine. However, I learned a while ago that it is truly impossible to maintain straight A's in technical subjects without serious computer assistance. Things are moving so fast that, in order to just stay even, you need all the help you can get. Instead of taking time to go to the library, I had to train my computer to go for me. While I'm doing math homework, for instance, it may be riding the Internet looking for source material for a genetic engineering project. As it collects information, it reduces it to a topic tree. I inspect the tree from time to time and make adjustments that gradually steer the system toward the input I really need. Systems like mine are not toys, they are truly necessities. It took me about 30 minutes to collect and analyze all of the publicly available information on Wonder Enterprises and distill it down to about 50 pages on my PDA," he said, taking the calculator-sized device out of his attaché case.

"Years ago," Mark continued, "I understand that many people viewed the telephone with great suspicion—amazingly the computer is still viewed that way, at least in some quarters. One of the things I learned with what you call my 'toys' is that competitors are gaining ground on Wonder. Evidently, they are modernizing aggressively, especially in customer service."

"I'm sorry Mark," the old man replied. "I evidently know less about your world than you seem to know about mine. Maybe I should shut up and listen. First though, tell me, this term 'knowledge worker' you keep using, what exactly does it mean? Who are these people?"

"Hey Gramps, no need to apologize. I'm just beginning to realize that what has been obvious to me and my friends for some time may not be obvious at all. Let me try to explain."

Mark started by explaining to his attentive Grandfather that just about everyone who works with information at any level is potentially a knowledge worker. However, those who do not, will not, or cannot share information with their colleagues are still likely to be called by old fashioned titles: administrative assistant, salesperson, research analyst, even vice president or CEO.

Mark went on to describe the evolutionary revolution that was in full swing and was changing office workers into knowledge workers. He described how communities of knowledge workers in academia and business had adopted cultures that made information central rather than peripheral to their operations. The provided systems support featured modern intuitive and responsive information handling capabilities. The first duty of the knowledge worker is to make information learned on behalf of the enterprise immediately part of the corporate knowledge base. In this way, information learned is not just remembered, it is also shared with fellow knowledge workers. Otherwise, without pervasive systems and a complementary culture, we are supporting an intellectual caste system whereby only so-called "creative people" are paid to think. As long as this situation prevails, other workers' thoughts related to product and process improvements can only be considered through the old fashioned Suggestion Box. With the right support system, each worker can become a knowledge worker with the capability to contribute and know everything that the enterprise knows, rather than just what they can learn as individuals.

"Imagine," Mark concluded expansively, "if you knew everything that your 500 employees knew and vice versa. You guys wouldn't have competition, you'd be unbeatable."

"Well, I can see that this would be a great theoretical solution to the George Formby problem and several others I can think of," responded Granddad, "But, is it really workable or merely Utopian?"

"The best analogy I have read about for this type of information system is society itself," said Mark with growing enthusiasm. "Access and the information itself should be available freely and in a timely manner to all—a sort of information democracy. Within the system, as in society, there needs to be a set of laws and a code of behavior which many begin to call 'citizenship.' The theory is that, much as citizenship as practiced by the majority of law abiding citizens makes society work, so does this other form of 'citizenship' make a corporate knowledge base successful. Folks who try to destroy, steal, or mutilate information are bad citizens. Bad citizens risk being locked out of the system rather than being locked up somewhere as in society. Others who take more than they give are not contributing members of society. In a sense, without the sort of system I am describing, you have information anarchy. This may be a strong word to describe the approach that has brought Wonder Enterprises this far. Nevertheless, you must see that it is a fair description in contrast."

"There is also a competitive issue here. Without a corporate knowledge base, the enterprise is an enterprise in name only. With an accessible institutional memory, it is an enterprise in fact as well. An enterprise must remember those things that make the enterprise work, or not. If they fail to do so, the enterprise becomes vulnerable to competition. The efficiency, pervasiveness, care and feeding, diligent exercising and use of the institutional memory is the key to corporate fitness. In the '80s someone said, 'The network is the computer' and that is true. Now people are saying that the network is the world and that the knowledge base is the enterprise."

"Well Mark, I'm impressed," said the old man, intrigued yet still skeptical, "but how do you get such a system going and, while we're on the subject, how do you keep it going?"

"That is an interesting question for you to ask me when you have built a business like this one," said Mark, somewhat taken aback. "However, I'll tell you what I know."

Mark explained that, just like every major undertaking, the implementation of a corporate knowledge system requires both sponsors and champions. Sponsors see the benefits and are moved to make the investments in enabling technologies and talent required to bring them about. Champions, on the other hand, are the needed talent. They will "sign up" to develop citizenship requirements, establish a culture, and, in short, make the system work. However, it has to be recognized that building a knowledge base requires what CAI/SISCo referred to in the '80s and '90s as *infocentricity*—a process whereby information is made central rather than peripheral to both knowledge worker activity and the enterprise.

Thought by thought, piece by piece, event by event, the base of knowledge will grow. The satisfaction derived by all involved provides the momentum needed to keep it going from day to day. As each day ends, the enterprise now knows, owns, and can share more information than it knew that morning. Similarly, participating knowledge workers also know more. Since all are involved in and dependent on both the support and ever-growing base of knowledge that the system represents, several other benefits accrue. First, a heightened loyalty to the enterprise emerges because of the investment that the enterprise has made in its people. Over time, the system will become self-policing, since knowledge workers tend to demand excellence of both themselves and their peers—they grow to resent sloppiness. Interestingly, peers are all other knowledge workers who, as already explained, include everyone up to senior management. Studies have shown that employee retention is enhanced, since no one would want to leave behind his or her memory, especially if it means having to build up another somewhere else from scratch.

Day by day, the enterprise's cache of intellectual capital will grow in value. Very quickly, it will overshadow other assets—buildings, machines, etc.—not just to the enterprise, but to most modern forms of valuation. In this, Mark was alluding to the fundamental accounting change that had been enacted to include information assets on corporate balance sheets. This had created a new set of Wall Street darlings who were known as the "information intensives."

"Yes, my broker urged me to jump on that bandwagon some months ago," said the elder Wonder. "In listening to her, it became obvious that not all who have tried—how do you say it—infocentricity succeeded. What do you know about that?"

Mark explained what he knew about some of the common mistakes that had led to failures as cited in his readings. One was to make an investment to acquire an infrastructure, boxes, wires, and software, for the desired environment, but to neglect cultural development. It must be remembered that the knowledge worker is the *alpha* and the *omega* of the corporate knowledge base. They supply the information for all to reuse as well as reuse that which they and/or their peers have prepositioned.

Another common mistake he had read about was deployment of a support system to provide only a one-way flow of information. Successful knowledge systems tend to draw the knowledge worker culture out of the user community. Unsuccessful systems serve only to draw data out of office workers, usually in support of what used to be called management information systems. Today, Mark pointed out, such information is recognized to be a mere by-product of knowledge worker activity rather than an end in itself.

Failure of sales-related knowledge worker support systems had been common. Mark was well aware of the natural reluctance that old-time salespeople had toward lead sharing, for instance, when leads were still often regarded as a form of currency. This tended to work against the philosophical change that infocentricity was all about. However, once enterprises faced the need to make corresponding changes to the ways in which people were motivated and compensated, sales oriented implementations began to flourish and grow. It made sense that if the sales-making capability of a group could be enhanced, the group would be able to eclipse the performance of an old-style, every-man-for-himself sales culture.

The last example of common mistakes Mark cited concerned scrimping on information technology to support knowledge workers. While a computer costs a small fraction of a knowledge worker's annual cost, it makes economic sense to enhance productivity by buying and judiciously maintaining the best and fastest systems support available. Penny-wise and pound-foolish is the enterprise that does not recognize that the real savings are in knowledge worker productivity, not purchase costs.

"Look at the time!" exclaimed Wonder Senior, "the morning is almost over and I haven't even begun showing you around."

CHAPTER FOUR

The Tour

Leaving the executive suite, they began a tour of the premises that started with the receiving dock area. Here, huge articulated trucks disgorged their palletized contents into a vast warehouse. Forklift truck drivers entered the trailers, emerging with load after load. Supervisors clad in khaki-colored lab coats examined crates bearing exotic markings, and noted serial numbers which were spoken into pedestal-mounted workstations. Once satisfied with the response from the system, the supervisors waved the forklift drivers on, speeding their loads off into the warehouse and their system-generated destinations.

"This system automatically updates available inventory and will spark a flurry of activity in the order department—they've been waiting for some of this stuff," said Grandfather Wonder. "We have had a devil of a time maintaining a supply of rubber chickens, this being an election year and all. The secret to our business is to strike the best balance we can between high customer satisfaction and average inventory levels. This means that sometimes customers have to wait a little for some items, but we aren't stuck holding a lot of novelties that don't move quickly."

They moved on through the warehouse, where forklifts and conveyor belts were active, and approached the loading dock area at the other end of the warehouse complex. Here, smaller trucks were being loaded with customer orders consisting of brightly colored cartons bound together by clear plastic. Pickers on airline-like luggage trains used computer-generated lists to develop specific orders with economy of movement.

"You know Gramps," Mark began, "handheld computers with built-in telephony could help your operation a lot. Radio frequency communications make it possible to bring the computer to the information instead of vice versa. You could also add bar code readers to them and cut out picking errors."

"Whoa! Steady on, young man," said the old man, "surely you're not suggesting we turn our warehouse staff into knowledge workers, are you?"

"Well, yes, I suppose I am," Mark replied. "There seems little sense in not putting the available manpower to its highest and best use. Besides, I'll bet that your warehouse staff could suggest some interesting improvements. Treating them as thinking human beings rather than mere laborers is sure to pay dividends in terms of progress and productivity. Surely, businesses like Wonder Enterprises are evolving from inventory-holders toward a situation whereby suppliers would ship directly to your customers. In that scenario, all of this disappears and electronic data interchange becomes the linkage for the 'virtual' wholesale operation. One step further than that, and the middle man disappears completely in favor of online product catalogs that can help anyone find anything, anywhere at its source."

"It sure seems as if you have 20/20 foresight, but this is only 2011," said the grandfather. "It sounds as though the world you describe is going to have to seriously redefine both work as we know it and the worker, too. Running this business without a warehouse and inventory would sure cut down costs. I suppose the factories that make novelties would still sell the same levels of goods—just in more and smaller transactions. Beyond the so-called 'virtual' wholesaler, factories will monitor retail inventories and ship automatically to maintain stocks at predecided levels. I see that, while everything is likely to change, it will also remain the same, at least in the fundamental respect that someone, somewhere will still be buying whoopee cushions and the other staples of our business!"

• • •

Away from the warehouse, they entered what Mark's grandfather described as the "heart" of the enterprise—the Disneyesque product development and testing shop. Here, new product ideas were dreamed up, prototypes built, and all products tested for quality, safety, and durability. It was a hive of activity with Disney-like characters, wearing long white coats and *pince-nez*, in various creative postures.

"Creativity is the business of this shop," the old man said gravely. "I'm confident in saying we spend more on product development and testing than anyone else in the novelty business."

"I certainly can't dispute that Gramps," Mark replied. "My analysis showed that you put the most into it, too. But what do you really get out of it?"

"What do you mean?" the old man responded incredulously. "Our attention to quality and safety is legendary."

"I'm sorry, Gramps," Mark replied. "I wasn't talking about those issues—I was talking about information. Where is all the information these people learn, think, and know stored? This place is alive with ideas and thoughts about new products, product improvements, new materials, etc. It is a veritable mine of creative information that is not captured. I know you value this information, but what I cannot fathom is why you don't even attempt to capture and remember it as a corporate asset."

Mark sensed that he had hit an exposed nerve with his admonition and sought to change the subject. "Did you hear the one about the woodsman and his encounter with the first chain saw?"

• • •

They moved into the office areas. They stopped first at the purchasing department. The waiting room was full of salesmen trying to see Wonder buyers to interest them in the latest item. Mark couldn't help but be fascinated with the thought that one of them might be trying to promote the Hula Hoop of the century or some other "next big thing." Buyers pored over sales and inventory level reports, huddled over desks with vendor representatives, or were involved in prolonged negotiations over prices and schedules with suppliers.

Next, they went through the sales department. Here, the rubber met the road in terms of selling what had been stockpiled in the warehouse. It was a hive of activity. Suspendered salesmen gesticulated to unseen customers over handheld telephones. They cajoled and persuaded unseen yet reticent customers about the virtues of promotions, bundles, and economic order quantities. This was the pre-Christmas buying season.

"Taiwan is our largest source of suppliers," said Wonder Senior, "followed by China proper." He had kept up a well-practiced monologue, well populated with corporate statistics that demonstrated an encyclopedic knowledge of the enterprise.

Mark consulted his PDA.

"No, it isn't," Mark said.

"No, it isn't what?," replied his Grandfather, visibly annoyed at the interruption.

"No, Taiwan isn't your largest source of supply," Mark responded. "It was in 2002, but last year Mexico became your dominant supplier source, at least, according to your SEC filings. Taiwan is now number three and China remains second."

"Show me that thing," said Wonder Senior, and after studying the PDA for a moment added, "I hate to admit it, but you're right. . .again."

"You know," said Mark, "there are some other things that I would like to point out to you. Those hand-held phones are a thing of the past. If you integrated the phone into their computer systems, your salesmen would be well on their way to becoming knowledge workers. They should be anchored to the system and be recording everything that their customers are telling them, about what sells and what doesn't, what their competitors are doing, and how they feel about the next season and the future beyond. Your customers are your antenna. As things are, only your salespeople learn these things, and, by-and-large, there is little that they can do with the information. However, if they captured its *essence*, it could be shared with the buyers, who would know a little of what may be happening and why, to add to their knowledge of what has happened and is happening."

• • •

Leaving the departments charged with buying and selling novelties, the old man and his grandson toured Wonder Enterprise's "back office" environments. Here, workers performed tasks such as managing payroll, personnel, customer billings, accounts receivable and accounts payable.

"The computer systems that support these operations can produce customer lists, rank-ordered by sales of a particular product, in an instant," said the old man rather proudly.

He approached an unattended workstation, pulled up a menu, and inexpertly filled in some query fields.

"There, just as I thought" he proclaimed proudly as the screen responded, "Gags 'R Us tops the list for plastic tarantulas."

"But," he added after further interaction with the workstation, "they are nowhere in the Top 10 buyers of green slime. I often wonder, no pun intended, why that is."

Mark knew that the mainly historical counting activities that supported his grandfather's demonstration were where business computing had started. For the best part of forty years, the world had written and rewritten thousands upon thousands of payroll and inventory control systems. In Mark's mind, this problem had been oversolved to the point where it held little interest, a sort of boring yet necessary evil. Nowadays, companies relied on a handful of packaged software vendors to provide modular solutions to suit the prevailing environment. The world had well solved the problem of counting money and objects, statutory reporting requirements, and the other trappings of operating an enterprise within a modern society.

Like Mark, Wonder Senior was not the "back room" type either. His interests lay with the people and products that made up his business. Sensing that Mark had a similar disinterest, he sought to deftly bring the tour to a close.

"Mark, do you remember what we always used to say was your favorite subject in grade school?" asked the grandfather.

"No, what?" Mark replied.

"Lunch," said the old man with a twinkle in his eye. "Let's get some."

CHAPTER FIVE

Luncheon Is Served

Mark and his Grandfather left the "back office" area and headed to the company cafeteria. It was by now almost twelve thirty, and the place was busy. As they made their way through the vast eatery, Wonder Senior acknowledged several people.

"Mark, this is Joe Frager," he allowed in his usual affable manner. "Joe, this is my grandson Mark. He has taken time from his busy college schedule to tell us what we've been doing wrong all these years," he said mischievously.

And then to Mark, "Joe has been with us for forty-two years. In fact, almost since the beginning."

Then to Joe, "Those were the good old days, eh?"

They moved on, entering a modestly sized ante-room. Here, in contrast to the main cafeteria, tablecloths were in evidence and the tables were set restaurant-style with cutlery, napkins, water glasses and a fresh flower in a small vase. They were greeted by a steward dressed in a white jacket. The steward led them to a corner table from which he deftly retrieved a "Reserved" sign as they were getting seated.

The steward explained the available fare, took their orders, and retreated.

The ante-room was quite busy. At some tables, Wonder buyers haggled with would-be product salespeople. At others, Wonder marketeers entertained buyers from customers or would-be customer enterprises. Wonder Senior excused himself and approached one of the tables. He stood talking with the diners, beaming all the while.

Mark began to think about what he had seen. He was struck by the realization that the entire "back office" setup amounted to a corporate memory of sorts. However, this memory tended to support primarily computational issues rather than the less tractable and, to Mark's mind, more important, informational ones. Business capital reigned supreme while, elsewhere in the organization, intellectual capital was being ignored. The "left brain" of the enterprise, counting things and money, was nurtured while "right brain" knowledge-based activity was largely ignored. Curious, Mark thought, since the family had long thought of them- selves as having a fairly artistic/creative orientation in pleasure and business.

"Well, what do you think?" asked the old man when he returned to Mark, obviously pleased with the energy that was evident in the room. "This is the sort of energy that makes a business pump," he added.

"Well Gramps," Mark started, "Clearly you have built a wonderful—excuse the pun—business that thrives. I have my thoughts on what I have seen, some of which I have already shared with you. But I have no right to criticize what you're doing and, frankly, I don't want to be seen as the Smart Alec."

"Mark, come on, let's have it," Wonder Senior replied in a conciliatory tone. "You have already given me some wonderful ideas. In fact, I think I have become what you called a 'sponsor' of change, maybe a disciple of infocentricity, even."

Mark sighed, "Well, I guess you asked for it. I hate to keep bludgeoning you about information, but that's what I understand best."

Mark shared his observations about the paradoxes inherent in the "back office" systems. He went on to describe how businesses in the '80s and '90s had been blindsided by change and so-called paradigm shifts. He told his grandfather that, according to his professors, this blindsiding had occurred when those who had built the products, organizations, and systems that were the organization's life blood were also charged with ensuring that their businesses prospered.

Mark went on to describe how in the '80s and '90s, the behemoths of the so-called "information technology" business had fumbled around with the essence of computing. Finally, they came to realize that the infocentricity concept was their future. The world had failed to beat a path to their proprietary architectural doors, realizing that the door was to a prison rather than a future, and the giants had subsequently failed at commoditizing low-cost raw computing power. Then they finally recognized that the real future lay not in making hardware, but providing the whole package that converts office workers into knowledge workers. This revolution took hold in about 2000, and the health of the industry began to change.

When the old man asked Mark what his intentions were with respect to Wonder Enterprises, he replied:

"Gramps, I have three hands. On the one hand, it would be wonderfully—pun intended—easy to step into a ready-made future. I could easily convince myself that I would be crazy to do otherwise. On the second hand—no pun intended—in conversations with my college counselors and fellow students, the consensus is to look for a future with an employer that practices infocentricity. If you don't, so the wisdom goes, you are forced to start it from scratch which, while arguably rewarding, is never the path of least resistance. How, they ask, can you make money without pre-positioned information?" He paused to eat some soup.

"My Knowledge Worker professor from last semester says that implementing infocentricity puts him in mind of this quote from T.S. Eliot's *The Cocktail Party*:

> 'The destination cannot be described; You will know very little until you get there. You will journey blind. But the way leads towards possession of what you have sought for in the wrong place.'"

"Of course," Mark continued, "he is one of those to whom everything suggests a quote from T.S. Eliot!"

"Very interesting," said the old man, "but you still, I believe, have one hand yet to go."

"Ah, ever the salesman Gramps, pressing for the close," observed Mark. "Well," he continued, "while it is true that, frankly, I don't yet know what I want to do, the challenge of taking the family business into the future is not unappealing. However, if I were to elect to do that, I would want the authority to turn the organization inside out, at least in an informational sense. The best way to learn about any enterprise, I'm told, is to look at the information. Once you discover what information is needed, used, or never available, you know what's important. Then you can set about trying to provide it in an accurate and timely fashion. Of course, all the while, one must avoid creating an 'information landfill.'"

"Should I take your answer as a firm maybe?" observed the grandfather. "I know there's no point in pressing you now, so instead, tell me, what in the name of heaven do landfills have to do with information?"

"Well, Gramps," Mark replied, "I'm afraid that not all office workers make good knowledge workers. If you're not selective, and if you don't train, you'll be violating Napoleon's hiring code and probably end up with a landfill where the stuff your people really need is obfuscated by a sea of garbage, you know, like a landfill."

"Yes, yes," said the old man impatiently, "I see what you mean about landfills, but what on earth does Napoleon have to do with this?"

"I'm sorry Gramps," Mark said with a grin, "I thought everyone older than me knew about the way Napoleon was said to have selected personnel for his armies."

Mark took out his PDA. He drew this nine celled matrix.

ATTRIBUTES	Lazy	Industrious
Intelligent	Generals	Field Officers
Stupid	Foot Soldiers	

"Now," said Mark. "it's very simple. The lazy/intelligent ones Napoleon favored as his generals, the intelligent/industrious ones he took as his officers, and the lazy/stupid ones he used as his foot soldiers."

"All right," said the old man, "I'll bite. What did he do with the stupid/industrious guys?"

"Nothing," replied Mark laconically. "He wanted nothing to do with them and neither does anyone trying to implement infocentricity because they are the ones that will create an information landfill."

They left the dining room and returned to Wonder Senior's office suite.

While Mark's grandfather attended to some business matters and returned some calls, Mark busied himself with his PDA. Using his icon library, he quickly developed two graphics. One was a pictorial representation of what he had observed during his tour. He labeled this "The Need for Infocentricity." The other was a sketch of what he believed Wonder Enterprises could become. He called this one "The Promise of Infocentricity."

Once his grandfather was free, Mark explained what he had done.

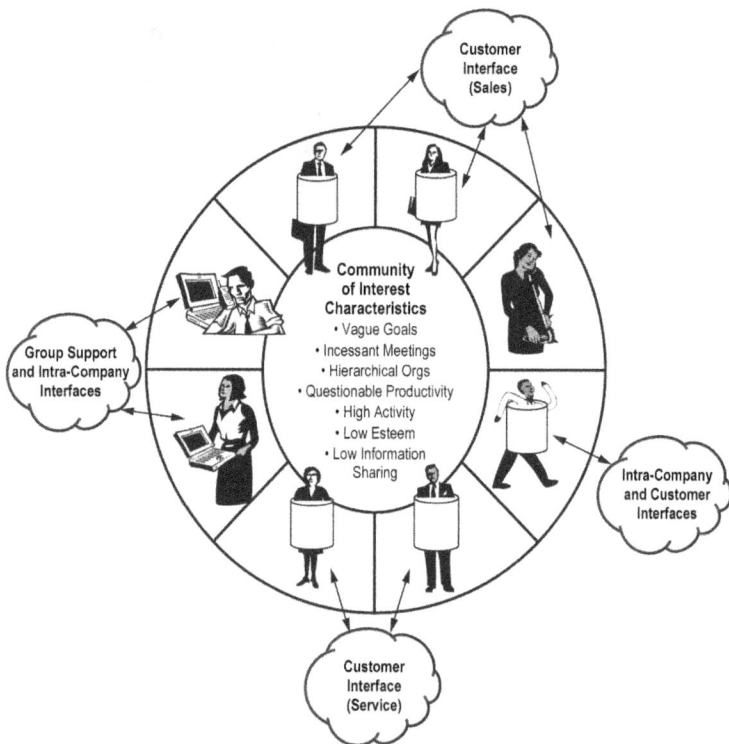

The Need for Infocentricity

"Today," Mark began, "the enterprise is the employees, and the employees are the enterprise. And for all sorts of crucial information, people are the only sources of information and the only corporate memory. As the first graphic tries to point out, people are forced to become the equivalent of databases that provide mobility, intelligence, and limited interaction with the other human repositories that make up Wonder. What's worse is that, as memories, people represent questionable reliability—they get sick, retire, or take other jobs. What then of a corporate memory built around people?"

Mark paused to summon the second graphic.

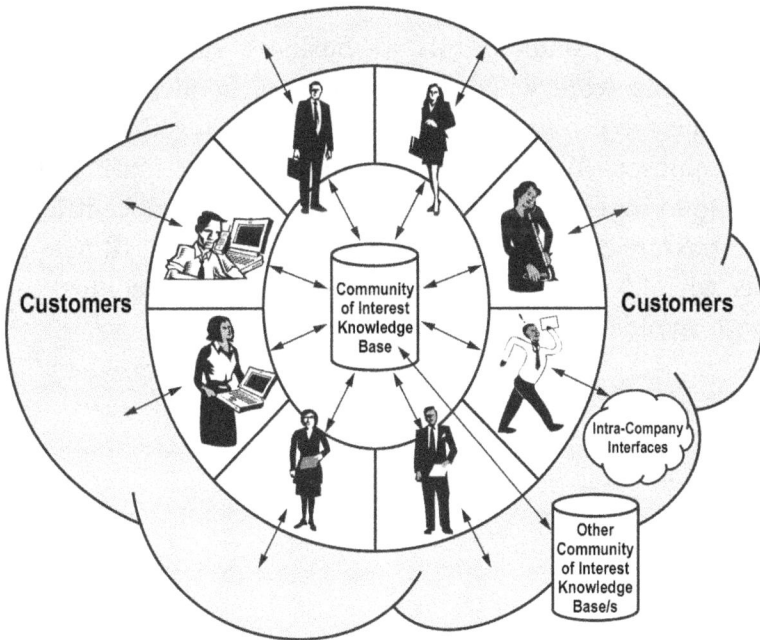

The Promise of Infocentricity

"Contrast that," he continued "with an enterprise that strives to record, remember, share, and reuse everything its people learn. For instance, in the dining room, most of your people weren't even taking notes. Not only will they forget most of what was said, your enterprise will learn even less. We need to develop a culture that values information and an environment where people think while machines remember and share the contents of the corporate repository. With information, there should be few barriers. We should offer to remember customer information too—all part of the service. If we are able to create the knowledge worker culture and infocentric support system I'm talking about, we should easily be able to find out why Gags 'R Us is not in your Top 10 buyers of green slime and hundreds of questions you haven't even asked yet."

"I like the sound of this 'we' business," said the old man. "I hope to work with you one day, the sooner the better. Perhaps we can accomplish your Nirvana together—I'll be the sponsor, you'll be the champion. In the meantime, I'm going to have our computer people look into infocentricity. Rest assured, I'll be asking some hard questions. I'd hate to see what I have struggled to build fall victim to a competitor with an older or smarter grandson."

CHAPTER SIX

The Moral

They drove home, each lost in his individual thoughts.

Mark knew that infocentricity was not a "plug'n play" proposition. Software publishers had already made that mistake in the '80s and '90s until they realized that implementation required a *cultural* change that, while initially painful to some, was ultimately beneficial to all.

Mark also knew that infocentricity can and should start modestly and expand in a cellular fashion and that it is an active capability—definitely not passive or purely reactive. As a concept, it can easily change your working life and the individual's entire approach to all forms of information. He knew the warm feeling that comes from knowing, as each day ends, that he now owns and can easily summon more relevant information than he could have that morning. Moreover, he knew about infocentricity's ability to increase productivity, lower overall costs, and sort the knowledge workers from the drones. In short, Mark knew infocentricity to be an intelligent and intuitive way of working that could enhance employee satisfaction and retention.

Mark also was aware of the predictions that the information pundits had made at the inception of the infocentricity era in the early '90s. They had said that, by the end of that decade, enterprises of all sorts would be moving forward with infocentricity, and, they would never go back, because:

- infocentricity would be the basis of all knowledge worker activity;

- the best help would soon demand pre-positioned tools and information; and

- it would be a major growth area for information technology systems and service providers.

Wonder Senior, for his part, was thinking about the future too. If he were to leave a "real" legacy, it was going to be in terms of information. He decided it was time to invest— he vowed to start the next day. He would order a computer for his desk. "Why stop there?" he thought, "I'll get one for home and one for the car, too. No more paper faxes for me. Over time, I'll record all that I know—thoughts, ideas, notes. . .the lot. From now on, I'll become a knowledge worker and inspire my peers to do the same. With a modest sustaining investment, which I can see will reduce over time, I could become both a sponsor and a champion. Over time, benefits will increase until. . ."

• • •

"Well thanks, Gramps," said Mark as they drew up to his house. "I know you must think I'm some sort of Smart Alec, but I really did appreciate seeing the business. Perhaps I can spend some more time there soon and see how infocentricity is helping."

"No problem, Mark," was the response. "Any time, the sooner the better."

"I guess," the old man continued slowly, "I have learned something about my business today that I thought I already knew."

"What's that?" asked Mark as he got out of the car, closed the door and leaned back in through the open window.

"Everything," was the reply.

Mark recognized that he had witnessed an epiphany.

"Who says you can't teach an old dog new tricks?" he said to himself as he entered the house and the rest of his life.

• • •

The End (of the beginning?).

www.ingramcontent.com/pod-product-compliance
Lightning Source LLC
Chambersburg PA
CBHW071125210326
41519CB00020B/6426